THE
HANDPRINT
OF
GOD

HISTORY OF THE HOPEWELL NETWORK

LISA BETZ & LESTER ZIMMERMAN

We dedicate this book to the memory of Jonathan (Johnny) Stoltzfus, who passed on to his eternal reward on July 27, 2017. Johnny and his wife Lilly took part in four revivals during his lifetime, including the Hopewell Revival which birthed the Hopewell Network. He carried a strong passion for revival and prayer in his spirit, and a deep love for the lost in his heart—may these live on in successive generations.

Hopewell Network
565 Airport Road
New Holland, PA 17557
HopewellNetwork@petra.church
www.HopewellNetwork.org

REL108020 RELIGION / Christian Church / History

ISBN 978-0-9992848-0-3

Contents

Prologue

As God continues to work from generation to generation, he always builds on the history of what has gone before. Those who believe the next, new move of God stands on its own and has no connection to what God has done previously make a huge mistake. It is imperative for those in ministry to understand the history of both the Christian Church as a whole and also the particular church or group they are a part of.

When God births a work he deposits a certain DNA or life seed into the foundation of that ministry. The future success of the work—even generations later—is tied to the original vision and DNA. If future leaders stray too far from the original purpose and core values God deposits into the foundation, the work will struggle in its identity, purpose, and anointing. Methods, styles, and ministries must change with the times, but the original core values must continue to guide the work.

With this truth in mind, the Network leadership has assembled the following brief history in order to assure a strong anointing and life flow of the Spirit for generations to come.

The Origins of Hopewell

Sometime around 1918, the pastor of the struggling Caernarvon Baptist Church, located between Elverson and Morgantown, PA, offered the building to the nearby Conestoga Amish Mennonite Church. The bishop of Conestoga had already been praying for God's vision for his congregation and decided the building was God's answer.

In June of 1920, two members from the Conestoga congregation began holding afternoon "Sunday School" sessions at their new church building, which was known locally as the Rock Church. Afternoon Sunday School sessions were a fairly common method for churches to perform community outreach in those days, but the local Amish and Mennonite congregations were not usually so outreach-minded. From its beginnings the Rock Church was proof that God was planning something new in the Morgantown-Elverson area.

The community responded, and before long evening services were added. The building had no heat, so it was only used in the warmer months, but despite being closed every winter an average of almost 80 people attended meetings at the Rock Church by 1933.

In April of 1936 the first Sunday morning service was held at the Rock Church. The congregation of forty-five members was officially organized a month later, with the support and oversight of ministers from Conestoga Amish Mennonite Church. Christian J. Kurtz, a minister from Conestoga, was appointed the first full-time minister of the Rock Mennonite Church in 1948.

At that time, the Rock Church belonged to the Atlantic Coast Conference of the Mennonite Church. The Mennonites, like the various Amish and Brethren denominations, came out of the Anabaptist movement.

The Old Rock Church
Photograph courtesy of Gwyn Groh

The Anabaptist Movement

The Anabaptist story goes back almost 500 years, to the time of the Protestant Reformation. The fathers of the Anabaptists felt the reforms of Luther, Calvin and others were not enough. These new Protestant churches were still controlled by the government, but the Anabaptists wanted complete freedom to worship as they saw fit. They broke away from state-sponsored churches to embrace a radical idea: the local community of believers, empowered by the Holy Spirit, was called to share the Gospel and work for authentic transformation in their community.

These radical Christians were called *Anabaptists* because one of their key distinctives was they rejected infant baptism in favor of believer's baptism. Since many of them had been baptized in their infancy, they chose to be re-baptized as believing adults. Hence, their enemies called them *Anabaptists*—"re-baptizers."

The early Anabaptists experienced powerful expressions of the Holy Spirit displayed through miraculous healings and divine protection. This power took ordinary men and women and turned them into dynamic preachers and teachers.

The Anabaptists had a practical faith, with the primary focus on simple obedience to scripture, rather than debates over the finer points of belief. Even today there is no single defining set of beliefs, doctrines, and practices that characterizes all Anabaptists, but they share a deep and rich faith, undergirded by spiritual humility.

The Anabaptists also embraced suffering. The Catholics, the Protestants, and the European governments all disapproved of the Anabaptist doctrines. Because their movement was unsanctioned, those who adhered to it were often actively persecuted—hunted down and killed for their faith. Yet they walked with courage, obeying the call to spread their message of God's love despite the fact their obedience might bring torture and death.

Many were burned at the stake for their beliefs. In the midst of burning fire they challenged those who were left to remain faithful. They did this with joy on their faces and songs on their lips. Their witness in death was so powerful that authorities clamped devices on their tongues at their public executions so that they could not speak.

Eventually, however, they wearied of persecution. Many Anabaptists made deals with governments in which they promised to forsake their evangelistic ways if they would be allowed to worship freely and live in peace. They became the "quiet in the land" and they lost their power. The movement became a culture.

Today God has rekindled this fire in people's hearts, with dreams of a church that embraces radical obedience, Holy Spirit empowerment, and willingness to suffer for the Gospel's sake. These people are passionate about intimacy with Jesus Christ and being a healing, transformative presence in local communities. They seek to reflect the local culture and customs, while refusing to bend from radical obedience to Scripture.

A New Building for a New Era

By 1971, the congregation at Rock Church was considering the need for a new building, with more room and updated facilities. One of the elders on the building committee, Wilmer Kraybill, had recently acquired a parcel of land just a mile from the current building. He and his wife, Helen, agreed to sell 2.6 acres of land to the congregation for the price of one dollar.

The building committee was determined to build the finest building possible: It would have the best windows, a paved parking lot, and be faced in stone. The faithful—but not necessarily wealthy—congregation gave their pennies and dollars to the building fund because they believed that the new building would enable many to be born into God's Kingdom.

The new church, renamed Hopewell Mennonite Church because the building was situated on Hopewell Road, was dedicated on May 12, 1974. At its dedication, the congregation consisted of twenty-two families, most of whom lived in the Morgantown-Elverson area. At the new building's dedication the congregation prayed, "We set apart this house to the worship of God the Father and to the service of our Lord and Savior Jesus Christ. Here shall the Gospel of Christ be proclaimed and taught for the salvation of men and the nurture of saints. May many be born into the kingdom here continuously until the Lord comes again."

The New Buildling
Photograph courtesy of Mark Kraybill

While the congregation was collecting funds for their new building, J. Edward Kurtz became senior pastor. Pastor Ed had strong ties to the church since both his father and grandfather had served as Sunday school superintendents. Pastor Ed suspected there might be more to the Christian life than he had heard and experienced so far. He had a vision for a church that was not a showcase for saints but a hospital for wounded souls—a place where hurting people could come and be accepted.

His vision led to changes, some of which reflected struggles happening within the larger Mennonite church, such as the acceptance of "worldly" vs. "plain" clothes and discontinuing the practice of segregating the congregation during worship—men on one side and women on the other. Pastor Ed also introduced baptism by immersion, rather than the traditional pouring, and the singing of simple scripture songs along with the traditional hymns (both sung a cappella). This last change was popular among the younger members of the congregation.

Pastor Ed opened the church to young people from Twin Valley High School, who began coming down to the old Rock Church for Bible study and fellowship. This was the first of several significant moves of God among young people within the community.

Pastor Ed's search for more of God led him to discover what was called the baptism of the Holy Spirit. At that time there was little teaching about the Holy Spirit within Mennonite churches, but once Ed and his wife, Helen, were introduced to the Holy Spirit's healing power they were eager to learn more. Ed became involved in Full Gospel Businessmen's meetings and sought the counsel of other church leaders who could answer his questions regarding the working of the Holy Spirit.

At about this time, Ed and Helen visited Strawberry Lake Christian Retreat in Minnesota. This center, founded by Gerald Derstine, brought charismatic pastors from many denominations to teach about the Holy Spirit.

The Loman, Minnesota Revival
(Sometimes Called the Strawberry Lake Revival)

In 1954 a group of pastors from Mennonite mission churches in Minnesota agreed to fast and pray one day each week for revival in their churches. As that year came to a close, youth from the nearby mission churches gathered for the annual midwinter "Vacation Bible School" led by Gerald Derstine and other local mission church pastors.

Over the course of the five-day event, the Holy Spirit began to move among the youth with prophetic words, tongues, and other charismatic phenomena. After his initial shock, Pastor Derstine accepted these unexpected happenings as a fulfillment of Joel's prophecy quoted by the apostle Peter in Acts, chapter two:

> *"In the last days, God says, I will pour out my Spirit on all people. Your sons and daughters will prophesy, your young men will see visions, your old men will dream dreams. Even on my servants, both men and women, I will pour out my Spirit in those days, and they will prophesy.'" (Acts 2:17-18 NIV)*

From that beginning, the revival spread to the home congregations of these young people, including Pastor Derstine's church, and began what would become a major charismatic renewal within the Mennonite Church.

However, the Mennonite leadership in 1955 did not approve of these strange happenings. When Pastor

Derstine refused to cease talking of these things or admit some of the phenomena were of the devil, he was "silenced" by the denomination. After several years of ministry in Florida, Mr. Derstine returned to Minnesota and founded the Strawberry Lake Retreat Center in 1965. In a DL-Online article celebrating the center's fiftieth year, Gerald Derstine claims, "God told me, 'We're going to build buildings and they're going to come from all over the world and they're going to go fishing and we're going to feed them.'" [1]

By the 1970s, many among the Mennonite church had embraced the charismatic movement, some even claiming that the renewal brought them closer to their Anabaptist roots. Pastor Derstine was eventually "restored" as an approved minister of the Mennonite Church. Today an estimated twenty percent of all Mennonites in the United States and Canada are spirit-filled, including many who serve on the mission field, fulfilling the prophecy that the Strawberry Lake Revival would affect the entire world.

The Kurtz's visit to Strawberry Lake Retreat gave them further encouragement to seek the Holy Spirit's filling and leading in their own lives and in their church. Pastor Ed searched the scriptures for guidance on how to bring himself and the church to a place where all honor and glory would be given to God alone. Prayer and fasting seemed to be the answer, so he and his wife called fellow church members to regular fasting and prayer meetings, where they sought God, prayed for church members, and actively prayed for revival within their community. The weekly meetings had been going on for about a year when the congregation moved into their new building. Those Saturday evening prayer meetings laid the foundation for what God would do through Hopewell.

Unfortunately, not everyone in the church accepted their pastor's new beliefs about the Holy Spirit, or appreciated the other changes he had ushered in. At times Pastor Ed felt like giving up, but his wife encouraged him to continue, reminding him he was not to place his security in the approval of people.

However, in the spring of 1975, Pastor Ed began to feel that the Lord was releasing him from the pastorate at Hopewell Mennonite. He had been given a glimpse of God's vision for Hopewell and had helped to prepare the church for what was to come, but now his role was finished.

At his final Sunday as pastor, several words of prophecy were given. (The very fact that the congregation accepted prophetic words was yet another sign that the Holy Spirit was at work within the church.) One prophecy stated that the church's next leader would be a spirit-filled person. Another stated that the church was like a stagnant pool, but a spring would bubble up and soon water would flow, even across the road.

The Next Leader

While Pastor Ed was preparing to leave, God was preparing another leader to take the church into its next season: Merle Stoltzfus, who had served as assistant pastor of the Rock Church from 1963-1967 before leaving the area to attend Eastern Mennonite Seminary.

When it came time for Merle to graduate, and he faced the responsibility of pastoring, he realized he was lacking something. His search led him to a fuller understanding of the Holy Spirit and His work in the believer's life. As he later wrote, "It should be emphasized also that failure to recognize and honor the Spirit on either an individual or congregational level, is to largely miss out on what God is doing today. The flow of the Spirit provides the setting in which God works." [2]

Merle's new-found understanding of the Spirit enabled him to start a dynamic young adult group that grew to fifty people within a month, but sadly it also caused friction during his first two pastorates in Indiana and Florida. Roy S. Koch later reported in *Christian Life* magazine that despite impacting many individuals, Pastor Merle was unable to impart his new spiritual freedom to the congregations at large. After his second frustrating pastorate, Merle is quoted as saying:

> *"Humiliated and feeling I had missed my calling completely, we went back to our home, parents, and community as failures. Everything I had depended on, my education, my schooling, the gifts of the Spirit, had been stripped away."* [3]

Fortunately for Merle, God had bigger plans. Looking back on that time he reported:

> *"What I am saying... is that the Lord built Hopewell not on human strength. It is being built on brokenness and prayer. When we are willing to turn those areas of defeat and brokenness in our lives over to God, He will do something with them."* [4]

During this time Hopewell had a thriving young adult group of around twenty-five, including students from West Chester State College (now West Chester University). The group had been looking for an able teacher who was young and relatable, so they asked Merle to lead their Bible study.

Merle taught the young adult Bible study for about six months. Then, in June of 1975, the Hopewell elders asked him to become pastor of the church. Pastor Merle shared his predecessor's vision for a church that was less legalistic and more open to the working of the Holy Spirit, but he had a style that was unique. He was a risk-taker for God, and that trait was evident from the very start. He accepted the elders' offer, provided they would agree to some fairly significant changes, including:

- The introduction of instrumental worship music (the Mennonite tradition was to sing a cappella). Dean Landis, a musician and graduate of Elim Bible Institute, was asked to be the church's first worship leader.

- The separation of baptism and church membership. Traditionally, a convert had to study the Mennonite Confession of Faith and agree to the responsibilities of active church membership before being baptized. Pastor Merle saw this as a hindrance for new believers.

- The introduction of a simple church covenant instead of the traditional church membership, which included a longer list of stipulations. (See Appendix 1 for a copy of the original covenant.)

- Switching from the *King James Bible* to a more modern version. Pastor Merle favored the *Good News Translation* (first published in 1966 as *Good News for Modern Man*), which in the early 70s was one of the most approachable versions available.

- The introduction of small home Bible study groups. Pastor Merle saw small groups as an important tool for discipleship, a belief that remains one of Hopewell's core values.

When he accepted the position, Pastor Merle made it known he believed in the gifts of the Holy Spirit. He was passionate about renewal within the church, but he was also diplomatic, able to work together with the congregation even when he encountered disagreements. Pastor Merle exhibited a humble style of leadership. He had a servant's heart—to the point that he was sometimes mistaken for the janitor. Most of all, Pastor Merle was a gifted evangelist. He was courageous, taking every opportunity for one-on-one witnessing.

The congregation embraced Pastor Merle's passion for evangelism. They had built their church so that the "Gospel of Christ be proclaimed and taught for the salvation of men and the nurture of saints." They were ready to accept people who did not fit their safe Mennonite mold, and they proved it by regularly inviting visitors home for Sunday dinner after church. Many of the core families went further, taking new Christians into their homes, so that these godly families could both assist the young believers financially and give them day-by-day instruction in how to live a Christian life.

When Pastor Merle realized that sharing meals was a significant way to connect with new believers, he suggested the church hold regular fellowship meals after the Sunday Service. Not only did new believers enjoy those meals, they brought their friends. With Merle as a catalyst, the church began to grow. By the time his one-year trial period was over, the church had doubled in size. The following year it doubled again.

The really exciting times were about to begin.

*Pastor Merle Stoltzfus and Pastor Lester Zimmerman
performing a baptism at St. Mary of Providence.
Photograph taken from the Hopewell Directory*

The Hopewell Revival

One thing Pastor Merle did not change was the Saturday evening prayer meeting. Throughout all that was to happen, Merle and his wife, Esther, met every Saturday with others from the congregation who had determined to pray for revival in the valley. Many of these faithful men and women still meet today and continue to pray for revival.

As Hopewell grew, more and more local people came through the doors to visit. As one local remembers, "Merle didn't come across like other pastors." He listened. He cared. And people responded. New believers came to the Lord. People were healed. Marriages were restored. And many recommitted their lives to the Lord with a new zeal to serve him. As new believer Mark Nicolas explained, "Hopewell is a joyful place to be, and the harmony, peace, and love in the fellowship is so fulfilling that people can't stay away." Even such unlikely people as the proprietors of the Elverson Bar and Hotel.

John and Sandra Shantz admitted their life was a mess at the time, but they had no intention of attending a church. Then their teenaged daughter ran away with her boyfriend, bound for Florida. Members of

Hopewell heard about the problem and Pastor Merle went to visit them. As Sandra remembers, Merle came to the kitchen door and said, "We heard you could use some help." However his visit came in the middle of the lunchtime rush and they were too busy to talk.

Merle came back the next day. John and Sandra were desperate for help, so they listened. Merle had contacts in Florida from his previous church, and he offered their help locating the girl.

A week later John's daughter was found. Police put her in the custody of Merle's brother, Harold, who brought her back to Pennsylvania. The daughter was furious at being forced to come home, but shortly after her return she became convicted of God's reality and accepted salvation. John claims her total transformation was the first thing that really grabbed his attention—a proof that God was real.

The Shantzes were so grateful for Merle's help in finding their daughter that they began attending Hopewell. Being more used to bar clientele than godly Mennonites, they felt uncomfortable at first, but the congregation gave them love and acceptance rather than condemnation, so they came back.

Before long, the Shantzes were holding Bible studies in the bar. John and Sandra would share the good news about the gospel with any customer who would listen, then give Merle the names of anyone who seemed interested. With the Shantzes' blessing, Pastor Merle made regular visits to the bar to wander around and engage people in conversations.

Before long the Elverson Bar Bible Study grew to twenty, then thirty, then fifty people, including many who had previously been bar regulars. In addition, Merle began sending many new church attendees to their group because it was a safe, encouraging environment for new believers to learn about the faith.

Not everyone was pleased with these changes, including Kel Zook who lived in one of the hotel's upstairs rooms and served as part-time bartender. Kel came from a strict Mennonite background that had embittered him to God and the church—especially the Mennonite church. He wanted nothing to do with the Shantzes' new-found faith. In fact, during this time his relationship with them soured to the extent that he and his wife, Pat, abruptly moved out of the hotel—a move that was doubly painful because Pat was Sandra's sister. Although Pat began to soften towards Christianity as she watched the changes in her sister's family, Kel remained adamant. He still patronized the bar, but wanted nothing to do with Christianity and he refused to set foot in church.

After several months of their dual bar proprietor-Bible study life, the Shantzes decided to close the bar, transforming their establishment into a restaurant—one that did not serve alcohol. John admits having cold feet about this decision, but then Sandra was miraculously healed of severe rheumatoid arthritis. Seeing this as confirmation that he needed to be more serious about God, John continued forward with the plan to close the bar.

Since it was the only bar in town, some Elverson residents were none too happy about the bar closing. It became a spiritual battle that climaxed the night the bar was to close. John and Sandra were forced to leave that night to take their son to the emergency room. They returned from the hospital to find police outside the building. The patrons had gone crazy. They had destroyed the bar, making a huge mess and even throwing things into the street.

Once things settled down, John and Sandra rolled up their sleeves and got to work. Pastor Merle and Jim Evans, one of the church members, helped (they had been downstairs praying during the uproar), and by the next day the mess was cleaned up and the new restaurant was open for business.

The transformation of the Bar (complete with pool tables, pinball machines, and a jukebox blaring rock music) to a Christian restaurant (with tables for Bible studies and worship music playing in the background) became front page news in the local papers, which attracted the notice of Reading, and then Philadelphia papers.

However, the Shantzes new restaurant struggled to make ends meet, and the building owners threatened to sell the property to someone who would re-open the bar. The building was eventually sold in June of that year, but by then God had provided the Shantzes with a five-bedroom home for their family, where they continued to host a thriving small group Bible study ministry.

When the new owners attempted to reopen the bar, the town voted to remain dry. It remains dry to this day. As Sandra Shantz said, "That building's been claimed for the Lord, and it's going to stay for the Lord."

About a year after the bar closed, Kel and Pat Zook moved back to Elverson. Eventually, Kel agreed to accompany his wife to the church that had become such a huge part of the Shantzes' life. The moment he walked in the door he felt something he'd never experienced before. He wasn't sure what it was but he told his wife, "We are coming back!"

He later learned that what he'd felt was God's love, coming to him through the people that filled the church. A few weeks after that first visit, Kel and Pat accepted Jesus into their lives during a visit to John and Sandra's home. Not only had their lives been changed, but the damaged relationship with the Shantzes was restored.

Pat and Kel Zook have been faithful members of Hopewell ever since. Kel's biggest joy is serving as a greeter, so he can extend that same love he felt that first Sunday to others who visit the church.

As God continued to draw people to Hopewell, the church attracted more and more notice. A number of newspaper articles were written about what was becoming known as the "Hopewell Renewal Movement" or "Hopewell Revival." They were followed by articles in national magazines. Even the 700 Club did a story on what God was doing in the Conestoga Valley.

Sunday Morning Service at Hopewell
Photograph taken from the Hopewell Directory

As the news spread, more and more people began visiting Hopewell, curious to see for themselves. Attendance grew so fast that a fellowship hall was built in 1978, followed by a new, larger sanctuary in 1979 that had a seating capacity of 500. As Merle said, "If they can't find a seat, they won't come back. Let's build."

Mennonite Churches from other parts of the country began to take notice of what was happening at Hopewell. They wanted to hear first-hand how God was drawing the non-churched, so they began to invite representatives from Hopewell to their churches to tell them what God was doing and help them figure out how to begin renewal in their locations. Hopewell began to send out visitation teams, made up of church leaders and two or three couples who were new believers. John and Sandra Shantz were often part of these teams, and other congregations delighted in hearing their dramatic story, as well as the testimonies of other new believers.

The home congregation never tired of hearing testimonies either. During the Sunday worship services, Pastor Merle regularly invited people to share what God was doing in their lives. Such testimonies were, and still are, an important aspect of how Hopewell celebrates God and his working.

Another facet of the church's growth was the youth: both the young adult group, which continued to grow after Merle became pastor, and the youth group started by Jim Evans. When Jim left to begin the first outreach church the youth group's leadership passed to Charlie and Joyce Martin. One of their first challenges as leaders was helping the existing youth to accept newcomers, even though it changed the dynamics of "their" group. Fortunately, the values of outreach and acceptance that characterized the church as a whole filtered down to the youth, and the group grew both in numbers and in spiritual maturity. As Charlie remembers, "There was quite obviously a move of God within the Hopewell church and this anointing extended to the youth group as well."

Charlie and Joyce wisely broke the teens into smaller groups, purposely separating close friends to foster a wider circle of relationships. The student leaders of these groups met monthly to pray, encourage each other, and share concerns. They were truly concerned for the spiritual welfare of those in their group, which led to both accountability and discipline happening within the groups—so much so that the adult leaders rarely needed to get involved when problems arose. Charlie remembers, "Observing God at work in these youth, giving them opportunities to develop and mature spiritually was undoubtedly my greatest joy throughout these years."

The Charismatic Renewal Movement

The phenomenal growth happening at Hopewell was part of the Charismatic renewal movement that was taking place across the world. The word *charismatic* is derived from the New Testament Greek term *charisma*, meaning "gift." Charismatic theology espouses a belief in a spiritual experience subsequent to salvation commonly known as the baptism of the Holy Spirit. Charismatics hold that the manifestations of the Holy Spirit given to those in the first-century church may still be experienced and practiced today.

The Charismatic movement is an interdenominational Christian renewal movement that spread throughout the country in the 1960s, 70s and 80s. Though much of the belief and practice of the Charismatic Movement came directly from the Pentecostals, the mainline churches who embraced such belief avoided the "Pentecostal" label for both cultural and theological reasons. The Charismatic renewal spread into many mainline traditions and new non-denominational churches and networks were birthed around the Charismatic experience and theology. This move of God swept around the world. Today it is estimated there are more than five-hundred million Christians who ascribe to Charismatic beliefs.

Exponential Growth

More and more people were attending Hopewell, many driving quite a distance. As Pastor Lester Zimmerman remembers of those days, "There was a strong sense of the Lord's presence, passionate worship, and a contagious warmth and excitement that just drew you in. There was no hype and the teaching was very practical, connecting with both the seeker and older Christians."

By 1981 the new sanctuary was beginning to fill up. Many of those who were regularly attending Hopewell came from outlying areas. Pastor Merle encouraged those families living further out to form a small group with others in their area so they could more easily meet during the week. One such group, located in Spring City, was led by Jim Evans.

As the Spring City group grew, Jim began to sense that perhaps it was time to begin a new church, one that kept the values and beliefs of Hopewell but that could more easily serve the Spring City area. Pastor Merle and the other leaders agreed that starting a new church seemed like the logical next step, so they allowed Jim to try the idea.

The new church had its share of challenges, but Pastor Merle saw the potential to reach many more people in this way. He shared a new vision with the congregation: Where ten or more families lived in an outlying area and had a strong small group, they should consider beginning a separate church.

To help churches get started a contingent of mature believers from the home church would agree to join the launch of a new church, staying a few months, or sometimes longer, to support the pastor and core congregation. Like Hopewell, these new churches were characterized by an emphasis of the working of the Holy Spirit, new forms of contemporary worship, song writing, small group discipleship, and a passion to reach the lost in their communities.

Occasionally these newly planted churches didn't "take root." In one case, a group located in Coatesville attempted to join with a small, struggling Mennonite church to create a new church. The joint venture did not work out, and afterwards the leadership sensed God telling them, "Don't build on somebody else's foundation." From then on, they did not.

Over the next twelve years, a total of twelve outreach churches were started across four counties. Eight were planted by Hopewell Elverson and four from thriving outreach congregations. Elder Johnny Stoltzfus, who was involved in founding several of the outreach churches, remembers, "It was always exciting to work with new believers. There's an exciting dependence on the Holy Spirit with people who have either made their first-time commitment or have newly entered into the baptism of the Holy Spirit. Working with such people, it is often easier to hear what the Holy Spirit is saying because of the atmosphere."

Despite all the new churches being formed, the original Elverson congregation continued to grow, requiring two additions to the existing sanctuary in 1982 and 1984, followed by the construction of a new sanctuary with a capacity of 1,400 in 1987. The vision of those faithful few who gathered every Saturday night for prayer had spread to hundreds of new believers. As Truman Hertzler, a long-time member of Hopewell said, "Surely this is a special work of God. We who saw it unfold often had to quote, *'This is the Lord's doing; it is marvelous in our eyes.'"* (Ps 118:23 ESV)

An Example of God's Work: The Reading Outreach

The Reading outreach church was a good example of how God was orchestrating things through this time of church planting. John Shantz was working as a salesman for Sports Equipment Supply owned by Randy Kulp. When the company expanded to a new facility, the old building at 12th and Perry Streets in Reading was sitting empty.

The Saturday evening prayer group felt led to utilize the empty space to begin an outreach church in Reading. The Reading outreach team, which included the Shantzes, held their first evening service in December of 1981. Three ladies who attended the service said to the leaders, "Are you part of Hopewell Mennonite Church from Elverson? We've been praying you would come to Reading."

From that promising beginning, the church grew rapidly. The following April they began holding morning services. Before long, they were looking for a larger building, so they asked God for direction. One day a customer entered the sports equipment shop. He noticed the Hopewell softball team photo on the wall and asked Randy, "Do you know anyone who wants to buy a church?"

He referred to a church located in the center of Reading, a graceful stone building with stained glass windows, seating for five hundred, and a nearby public parking lot that was free on Sundays. Incredibly, the building had been vacant for two years.

After visiting this lovely church, the leaders attended a prayer meeting with Pastor Merle. All in attendance were asked to decide what purchase price should be offered. Everyone independently decided on the same amount. Surely God was confirming their plans.

However, when the leaders made the offer, the seller informed them that another offer had just come in. The Hopewell team refused to increase their offer, so they waited to see what God would do. Eventually the other agreement fell through and the seller accepted Hopewell's offer.

Things appeared to be falling into place, so long as they managed to collect the money in time. Alarmingly, one day before settlement they were still fifteen-hundred dollars short. But God had matters in control. That evening, while the Shantzes attended the Saturday evening prayer meeting, someone slipped an envelope under Randy Kulp's door.

The contents? Fifteen-hundred dollars. The Hopewell Reading Church held its first service at the new building in September of 1982, less than a year after its inception. As Pastor Shantz said of the rapid growth, "Reading was a miracle church."

When John Shantz accepted the role of pastor for the new Reading outreach church, he was honest with the congregation about his limitations and about how he was only able to preach by the help of God. Also—he admits—with the help of Pastor Merle's sermon notes.

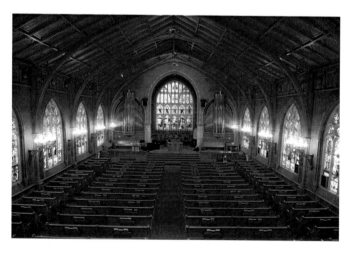

Interior of the Reading Outreach Church
Photograph courtesy Harry Yocum

Preparation, Prayer and Prophetic Promises

Before too long it became evident that leadership needed to give more time and effort into preparing pastors for ministry. They were willing to serve, but did not have the training typical for a pastor. In 1984 several Hopewell District leaders attempted to meet this need for more formalized training by developing the Hopewell School of Ministry, with Johnny Stoltzfus serving as dean. The school's purpose stated, *"The Lord has placed in the church many varied gifts and talents. It is the Lord's desire that those gifts and talents be exercised to bless His people. The School of Ministry is seen as an aide to shape and sharpen the use of those gifts."*

The school offered four majors: Leadership, Small Group/Discipleship, Worship, and Bible. For the next several years, this School of Ministry helped to train many eager-but-not-fully-equipped men and women, giving them a stronger foundation for their areas of ministry.

One person whose life was transformed by the School of Ministry was Becky Jones. After taking a class on prayer, she felt led to begin a regular prayer group to intercede for Hopewell and the many young churches that had been planted. Pastor Merle agreed to her vision, and asked her to lead a weekly prayer meeting that became known as the district prayer meeting.

Although she did not realize it at the time, Becky was taking over the intercessory work of Tom Miller, a founding member of Hopewell who had died the year before. Tom had spent many hours interceding for the lost and the work God did through the church. In addition to his faithful prayers, Tom also brought prophetic words, including the following: "The finances needed for all the district churches are already set aside in God's storehouse. The leaders need only ask God to provide and He will release what is needed to continue the work."

A year or so after establishing the district prayer group, Becky moved away from the area. Five years later, God led her back to Hopewell. "I had no plans to return to Pennsylvania," she remembers, "But God did, so he brought me back."

Before long she restarted the district prayer meetings. Shortly before the first meeting, she felt God giving her a word from the book of Haggai:

> "This is what the Lord Almighty says: 'In a little while I will once more shake the heavens and the earth, the sea and the dry land. I will shake all nations, and what is desired by all nations will come, and I will fill this house with glory,' says the Lord Almighty. 'The silver is mine and the gold is mine,' declares the Lord Almighty. 'The glory of this present house will be greater than the glory of the former house,' says the Lord Almighty. 'And in this place I will grant peace,' declares the Lord Almighty." (Haggai 2:6-9 NIV)

When she shared this word at the prayer meeting, a longtime intercessor from Petra Christian Fellowship, Mike Hollinger, affirmed the prophecy, saying God had given him the same word several years before. God seemed to be promising that although Hopewell's former glory during the peak of the revival was fading, God still had plans for Hopewell.

Transitions

Hopewell Mennonite Church was a member of the Atlantic Coast Conference of the Mennonite Church. Conference leadership was uncomfortable with some of the new things Hopewell was doing, but they couldn't deny that God was at work. To their credit they allowed Pastor Merle and the other Hopewell leaders to continue without interfering.

In fact, because of all the new churches Hopewell was planting, a new district was formed within the conference, with Merle serving as overseer. In doing so, the conference gave the Hopewell churches further freedom to follow God's leading without being stifled by conference forms or traditions.

Unfortunately, such sudden growth brought trials, as well as blessings, because God chooses to work through imperfect people. A lack of accountability, training, and structure began to surface, leading to burnout and other troubles. God began to bring problem issues to the surface during the district prayer meetings.

Serious leadership problems came to light, ultimately leading to Pastor Merle being released by the conference as pastor and district overseer in 1987. The

Hopewell District was shaken to its core, facing both a leadership vacuum and a period of uncertainty.

The sudden change threatened to tear apart what God had done. However, by God's grace, the majority of district pastors and churches pulled together and weathered the storm. Lester Zimmerman, lead pastor at Petra Christian Fellowship, was asked to take over leadership of the Hopewell district by both the district pastors and conference leadership. Lester and his wife, Erma, had previously pastored two churches in Baltimore Maryland before planting a Hopewell outreach church in New Holland. At this point he had the most experience among the Hopewell district pastors to provide the leadership needed.

It was immediately obvious that some significant structural changes were needed. Too many of the churches were led by a single pastor with little accountability or input from others. Lester assembled a team of leaders to act as oversight for the district then invited a team of spiritual advisors outside the district to provide accountability and counsel. This Spiritual Advisory Team consisted of Larry Kreider from DOVE International, Keith Yoder from Teaching the Word Ministries, and Dave Hess from Christ Community Church.

In addition, each of the Hopewell District churches was encouraged to become a pastor-and-elder-led church, with the Senior Pastor functioning as lead elder. Until this point, some of the outreach churches had not created an elder team at all, and those who had were not utilizing them effectively.

These changes reflected a general move among churches in America toward an apostolic or New Testament understanding of leadership and governance. Churches in this movement are often termed post-denominationalist, meaning these churches no longer fit into traditional denominational structures and agendas.

The Hopewell district took another step away from denominational-style governance in 2001. The Atlantic Coast Conference belonged to a larger organization known as the Mennonite Church, which was about to merge with the General Conference of the Mennonite Church to create the new Mennonite Church USA. Hopewell district leadership recognized that the larger Mennonite denomination was not heading in the same direction they were called to pursue, so they asked to be released from the conference.

The Atlantic Coast Conference graciously agreed to the request. At one of their conference meetings they laid hands on the Hopewell District Overseer Team, blessed them and sent them out—the Hopewell churches were no longer part of the Mennonite Church. During this significant time of transition, the overseer team consisted of: Lester Zimmerman, Victor Dunning, Ken Kirk, Allan Yoder, and John Shantz.

Thus was born the Hopewell Network of Churches, with Petra Christian Fellowship serving as the central office. The launching of this new network gave the Hopewell churches a fresh opportunity to identify the core values that would characterize the network.

They also created a more uniform set of bylaws to help maintain a united vision.

The leadership team (now called the Apostolic Team instead of the Overseer Team) decided to decentralize some of the decision-making and credentialing processes. They moved from the congregational model of governance to a more apostolic form of leadership.

Petra Church (formerly Petra Christian Fellowship)
Home of the Hopewell Network Central Office
Photograph courtesy of Lester Zimmerman

In a congregational model the entire congregation votes on most church decisions. In a New Testament church model, the church is not a democracy. The pastors and elders make most decisions. This approach is based on the idea that God directs his church through the leadership gifts he sets in place. The leaders, while open to congregational wisdom and discernment, are ultimately responsible for all decision-making.

The Apostolic team also developed an additional team of leaders with ministry gifts of Apostle, Prophet, Evangelist, Pastor and Teacher. This Five-Fold Ministry Team has been a tremendous help in discerning direction and providing ministry to the churches and leaders.

Continued Growth—Inside and Out

Church growth slowed during the years of leadership change and restructuring, but God was still moving. Four more outreach churches were started during this time (1987 to 2000). Growth occurred in other ways as well. Some members of the new generation were taking positions of leadership, as worship leaders, youth leaders, etc. Although their style was different, they continued on Hopewell's foundation of heart-felt, contemporary worship, song writing, and an emphasis on discipleship.

One of the new leaders was Curt Malizzi, who took over leadership of the School of Ministry when Johnny Stoltzfus began pastoring the Telford outreach church. As time went by, Pastor Curt realized the current school was no longer serving the needs of the district, so he developed an affiliation with Chesapeake Bible College and Seminary. Under Pastor Curt's leadership the School of Ministry was expanded, offering several accredited courses at Hopewell Christian Fellowship in Elverson and a number of outreach churches.

Over the years the school has experienced a natural ebb and flow, evolving as the needs of the churches had changed. Currently the network partners with DOVE International and offers classes nationally and internationally. Training continues to be an important value of the network. As a current edition of the

Network Values reads: *We have a vision to see leaders raised up and trained in both Scripture and ministry skills for church and marketplace.*

The school of ministry was not the only vehicle for training future leaders. In the mid-eighties, Dean Landis began developing a vision to see the churches work together in children's ministry. Since most of the churches were just beginning and rather small at that time, he decided the solution was to run day camps at the various churches. He took a small staff to each location to work alongside people from the individual churches.

After two or three summers of successful day camps, Dean and his team decided to begin an overnight experience, held at the Tel Hai Camp and Retreat facility in Honey Brook, PA. He remembers, "We were so amazed by how God openly moved upon the kids causing them to be caught up in God's presence for hours. Seeing them pray for each other and respond to God blew away all my expectations!!!"

Michael Guertin, who has directed Hopewell Summer Camps since 1991 adds, "Since I've been leading them our camps have mostly been grooming the young to spend long periods of time in the presence of the Lord and *ENJOY* it. Plus, camp has been a tool used by the Lord to rekindle youth who have 'heard it all' and have grown cold. Also, it has been an indispensable tool in the hands of the Lord to impart vision and hands-on training to countless youth and children's workers through the years."

Expanding the Network

Hopewell's transition to an independent network enabled new avenues of growth. Other churches began approaching the network leadership with requests to join the network. The Apostolic Team was cautious about admitting new churches, but after careful consideration they developed criteria to ensure that all new churches, local or international, share Hopewell's core values.

Today the network continues to grow as new churches are planted, existing churches are adopted, and international networks are added. The network presently consists of sixteen churches in the United States, plus many congregations belonging to international networks in Haiti, Kenya, Mexico, India and Thailand. (See Appendix 2 for a list of Hopewell Network Churches and International Networks.)

Before the network began partnering with international churches, the Apostolic Team sensed that God was calling them to adopt an unreached people group as a joint effort of all network churches. In 2005 the Apostolic Team, along with other key leaders, participated in a one-day retreat seeking God for direction. Where did God want to send them? After spending time in individual prayer the group gathered in front of a large world map. One by one, they each pointed to the country where they felt God was leading them.

Almost everyone pointed to the same country: Thailand. God was calling the network to the Issan people of Thailand.

Since the network adopted the Issan people as their joint mission focus, they have spent many hours in prayer over the region. The first team sent to Thailand, comprised of Pastors Dwane Reitz, Allan Yoder, Curt Malizzi and Lester Zimmerman, were tasked with refining the strategy. They discerned where the network should be serving and what their main focus was to be. The team arrived home with answers: They would go to the city of Ubon Ratchathani and focus on youth.

Next the network sent short-term prayer teams, whose goal was to prepare the way. Finally, the first long-term missionary team was sent in 2012, led by Keith and Carol Hershey. Since that time, other families have joined the work in Ubon. Lazaro (Nacho) and Merrilee Barrera and their family are presently leading the work in Thailand.

The Network's focus on Thailand may look like a new and different type of ministry, but it is based on the foundational value of evangelism—a value Hopewell shares with those first Sunday School efforts in the old Rock Church and, before that, its Anabaptist roots.

Re-Digging the Hopewell Well

Each ministry God births has a well or life-flow of the Spirit that feeds it. Over forty years ago, God opened a new well—Hopewell—which from the very beginning was dedicated to God through the founders' prayers: "Here shall the Gospel of Christ be proclaimed and taught for the salvation of men and the nurture of saints. May many be born into the kingdom here continuously until the Lord comes again."

However, over time these wells can get stopped up by traditions, struggles, and neglect. In Gen 26:18-19 we read:

> *Isaac reopened the wells that had been dug in the time of his father Abraham, which the Philistines had stopped up after Abraham died, and he gave them the same names his father had given them. Isaac's servants dug in the valley and discovered a well of fresh water there. (NIV)*

Sometimes in order to experience revival and a fresh move of God's Spirit a church or ministry must go back and unplug or re-dig the old wells, as Isaac did. He understood that he must first honor his heritage by unstopping the wells of his father before he began to dig wells of his own. Both are important. The old and new together bring strength and health to a ministry.

The significance of re-digging old wells is more fully explained in Lou Engle's book, *Digging the Wells of Revival*. He writes:

> I believe God is saying we can go to the wells of our fathers and dig again to find streams of revival bubbling forth. I am not speaking of re-digging a well to return to the traditions of the past, or to rediscover old methods or cherished doctrines. Rather I am talking of coming alive again with the waters of the Holy Spirit that were found in the wells of our spiritual ancestors. ... It is time we discover the ancient inheritances upon which the church was founded. It's time to clear out the wells of revival that have been polluted by divisions and the traditions of men. This is the season when sons and daughters can repossess the wells that their fathers and mothers fought to dig. The glory of God that bubbled up and spilled over in days past will again refresh God's people and bless them with the presence and power of the Holy Spirit that many have only read about and longed for. Men and women will again wear the mantles of the saints who fasted, and prayed, and

tarried until the glory of God came down. There's a well beneath your feet. Dig it, lest you die. ... God's counting on you to renew the covenants of your spiritual forefathers, to rebuild the ancient ruins, and to reclaim their prophetic destinies. [5]

Dutch Sheets explains this insight further as he reflects on his visit to Cane Ridge and Wales where there is a rich history of revival:

Scripture makes it clear that the Lord accomplishes His purposes on the earth not through one man or movement, but through the labors and legacy of many across multiple generations. (Heb 11:39-12:2). Working through a divine timeline that extends beyond a single lifetime, the Lord desires that we honor and build upon the foundations laid by those who have gone before us. In Genesis 26 we are told that when Isaac dug water wells, he didn't get to start with his own. Isaac recognized his hereditary right and responsibility to re-dig and restore the ancient wells of his father Abraham, which the Philistines stopped up after he died. It was after re-digging his father's wells that the Lord appeared to Isaac and pronounced over him the same blessing previously spoken over Abraham. Not long after that, the Lord allowed Isaac's servants to unearth his very own well. [6]

The Well's Flow—Past, Present, and Future

As we look toward the future, it is important to consider the Hopewell Network's DNA and the anointing we carry to bless the broader body of Christ. What is our life stream? What spiritual life feeds our historic wells that future generations can tap into? What inheritance and destiny can be rediscovered in a fresh way?

Here are some of the things that God has deposited in our well for future generations to walk in and expand upon:

1. **A passion for God's presence** – God's presence has always been more important than great worship, preaching or programs. At times his presence is so deep and real that nothing matters more than soaking it in. God's presence is our most valuable gift to steward and nurture.

2. **A passion to reach the lost** – God gifted Hopewell with a special ability to connect with and accept seekers and new believers. There is a unique ability to make room for the Holy Spirit and yet be sensitive to new believers at the same time. Reaching the lost is the main purpose of the church.

3. **Holy Spirit empowerment** – Hopewell was founded with a deep honor for and openness

to the Holy Spirit. The Baptism of the Holy Spirit is clearly taught and is a key to what God is doing. All the gifts of the Holy Spirit are embraced, and they enrich both our lives, churches, and our walk with the Lord.

4. **Relevant teaching from the Bible** – There is a deep respect for the full inspiration of God's word. The Scriptures are kept central. While the Bible is taught with authority, it is also taught with an emphasis on practical application that everyone can relate to.

5. **Worship and song writing** – Worship has always been an important and powerful part of our church life. Hopewell people have always loved to worship. In addition, there is a special anointing and grace to write songs that release God's prophetic purposes.

6. **Prophetic guidance** – There is a strong prophetic gift that is part of this network's spiritual DNA. We don't just run on good ideas, but decisions are bathed in much prayer as we wait for a clear word from the Lord.

7. **Healing ministries** – Hopewell has always been a safe place for hurting people. From the early days of our network, there has been an emphasis on healing ministries. A strong healing stream flows throughout the network churches, and we see many spiritual, emotional, relational, and physical healings.

8. **Persistent prayer** – Hopewell was built on a strong foundation of prayer, and over the years that heritage has remained strong through the steadfast efforts of many. There is a grace upon this network in the area of prayer—passionate, persistent prayer that fosters revival, breakthrough, and reaching the lost.

9. **Discipleship** – The ability to help people grow in the faith has always been a core value. We take the task of making disciples seriously. From the beginning, small groups have been a key part of discipleship.

10. **Planting new churches** – A church planting movement sprang forth from what God was doing through the Hopewell revival. God has given us a grace and calling for church planting nationally and internationally.

11. **Strong sense of community** – There is a deep fellowship among the people and among the pastors and churches. This creates a deep unity and a sense of united mission.

12. **An intergenerational focus** – Intentionally calling forth and equipping children, youth and adults.

Heritage, Past and Present – Our New Testament Foundations

The Apostolic Team has defined the mission of the Hopewell Network this way:

> *We are a fellowship of churches and leaders empowered by the Holy Spirit to locally and globally advance Christ's Kingdom together.*

> *We use the New Testament as our model and template for church life and governance. From the New Testament we see that the primary focus of the church is on the centrality of Jesus and his commission for us to reach the lost in the world around us.* [7]

Following are some foundational concepts that reflect our history and identity:

- A church built on Jesus Christ (I Cor. 3:11, Matt. 16:16-18)

- Authority of the Scriptures (II Tim. 3:16, II Peter 1:21)

- The primacy of the New Testament (Matt. 5, Heb. 1:1-3)

- Believer's water baptism (Mark 16:16, Matt. 28:19)

- The Baptism of the Holy Spirit and spiritual gifts (Acts 1, 2, l Cor. 12, 14)

- The healing presence and ministry of Jesus (Matt. 8:16-17, Mark 16:17-18)

- The ministry of all believers (I Peter 2:5-9, II Cor. 3:6)

- A strong commitment to evangelism (Mark 16:15, Acts 1:8)

- A New Testament form of church governance (Acts 4:11, Acts 14:23)

- Discipleship in daily living (Matt. 16:24-25, Matt. 7:24)

- Correction with compassion (Matt. 18:15-18, I Cor. 5:1-5)

- Living simply (Matt. 6:19-21, I Tim. 6:6-7)

- The church independent of the state (Acts 4:18-19, Rom. 13:6-7)

- Embracing the power and sufferings of Christ (Php. 3:10, I Peter 2:20-21)

- Living a lifestyle of love and peace (Rom. 12:14-21, Matt. 5:38-42)

Looking Ahead: Faith Declarations

In 2011, at a Hopewell Network pastor's conference, Apostolic Leader Lester Zimmerman prophetically declared over the Network of Churches a faith declaration that God impressed on his heart. This has been declared multiple times over the network over the years. He declared:

- Regular outpourings of the Holy Spirit all over our network, nationally and internationally.

- Weekly salvations becoming the norm in our churches as we engage our communities.

- Life transforming teachings of the Word and effective discipleship.

- Young pastors, leaders and teachers emerging in our network that are rooted and grounded in the Word and are able to articulate and defend their faith.

- Each generation receiving the empowering baptism of the Holy Spirit and taking the gifts of the Spirit outside the walls of the church to impact our communities.

- Young people full of the Holy Spirit rising up as a counter-culture with the power and anointing of Jesus all over them as they engage in the church and culture.

- A greater release of the healing anointing that rests on the network so that healings become commonplace.

- Evangelism and caring for the broken remaining central in all we do as we engage in outreach, mercy and justice ministries.

- A fresh release of prophetic worship, and for prayer to become a deep passion in all our churches.

- A new generation of missions and church planting.

- A growing sense of community among the network leaders and churches.

- Our churches to be places flowing with God's grace, and places where the Word is uncompromised, as we love people to wholeness.

Epilogue

May this book be a testimony to God's power, love, and faithfulness and may it inspire successive generations to seek God for a fresh move of His Spirit in their day. May chapters full of the acts of the Holy Spirit be added to this story as each generation discerns the times and seeks the face of God. May this hope-well continue to be a well of life and hope to the world for generations to come.

Pastors and Leaders from the
Hopewell Network Conference 2016
Photograph courtesy of Lester Zimmerman

Appendix 1:
Early Copy of Covenant Terms of Membership of the Hopewell Mennonite Church

1. That there be a genuine conversion experience and willingness to testify to it.

2. That some form of believer's water baptism be submitted to.

3. That the Scriptures, including both the Old and New Testaments, be accepted as the Word of God.

4. That attendance be on a regular basis.

5. That there be a willingness to give and receive counsel in the brotherhood.

6. That giving be on a systematic basis, with tithing as a goal.

7. That a lifestyle based on love be followed and cultivated.

8. That marriage and family ties be given
    priority:

    a. That husbands take seriously their respon-
        sibility for leading their homes, and over-
        seeing the spiritual welfare of their family.

    b. That women accept their Biblical role
        in a consistent manner, submitting to
        their husbands, dressing modestly, and
        cooperating with congregational leaders
        in worship services. We recommend the
        veiled head in worship as a sign of this
        acceptance.

    c. That marriage be accepted as permanent,
        and that every possible aid be given mar-
        riages experiencing difficulty.

Appendix 2:
Hopewell Churches and International Networks

(* Indicates this church is part of the Hopewell Network. Others have either closed or changed affiliation.)

*Hopewell Christian Fellowship (formerly Hopewell Mennonite Church)
> Location: Elverson, PA
> Date Began: 1974
> Original Pastor: J. Edward and Helen Kurtz

*Spring City Fellowship
> Location: Spring City, PA
> Date Began: 1981
> Original Pastor: Jim and Bobbie Evans

New Life Mennonite Church
> Location: Downingtown, PA
> Date Began: 1982
> Original Pastor: Merv and Ruth Stoltzfus

Hopewell Mennonite Church
> Location: Reading, PA
> Date Began: 1982
> Original Pastor: John and Sandra Shantz

*Petra Church (formerly Petra Christian Fellowship)
Location: New Holland, PA
Date Began: 1983
Original Pastor: Lester and Erma Zimmerman

*Hopewell Community Church
Location: Pottstown, PA
Date Began: 1984
Original Pastor: Ken and Sandy Kirk

L.O.V.E Christian Fellowship
Location: Birdsboro, PA
Date Began: 1984
Original Pastor: Charlie and Pat Haws

Hopewell Mennonite Church
Location: Bernville, PA
Date Began: 1985
Original Pastor: John and Sandra Shantz

*Hopewell Christian Fellowship
Location: Telford, PA
Date Began: 1985
Original Pastor: Jon and Laura Landis

Hopewell Christian Fellowship
Location: Paoli, PA
Date Began: 1986
Original Pastor: Mark and Carol Nicolas

Hopewell Community Church
Location: Fleetwood, PA
Date Began: 1989
Original Pastor: Linford and Flo Weber

*Good Shepherd Community Church
Location: Denver, PA
Date Began: 1991
Original Pastor: Jim and Joan Wetzel

*Immanuel Christian Fellowship
Location: Manheim, PA
Date Began: 1992
Original Pastor: Edgar and Naomi Sensenig

*Hope of the Nations Christian Center
Location: Reading, PA
Date Began: 2000
Original Pastor: Gustavo and Twila Ramirez

*Tierra Prometida
Location: Hagerstown, MD
Date Began: 2008
Original Pastor: Linker and Luz Sanchez

Second Chance Ministry Center
Location: Orlando, FL
Date Began: 2012
Original Pastor: Ralph and Mildred Estrada

*Freedom Path Church
Location: Akron, PA
Date Began: 2013
Original Pastor: Jim and Cathie Kearsley

*The Way Church
Location: Chalfont, PA
Date Began: 2015
Original Pastor: Jacob and Abigail Kim

*Pasion
Location: Lancaster, PA
Date Began: 2017
Original Pastor: Mario and Jeanette Araya

Adopted Churches

(* Indicates this church is part of the Hopewell Network. Others have either closed or changed affiliation.)

*New Freedom Church, Sudlersville, MD
*Kingdom Life Ministries, Hesston, KS
*Living Hope Fellowship, Forksville, PA
*Living Truth Fellowship, Christiana, PA
*Rockville Fellowship, Belleville, PA
Acts Covenant Fellowship, Lancaster, PA
Tree of Life Apostolic Ministries, Myerstown, PA
Lakeview Christian Church, Chestertown, MD
Faith Mennonite Church, Oxford, NJ
Cornerstone Celebration Church, Downingtown, PA

Hopewell International Networks

Grace Assembly of Churches
Location: Port-au- Prince, Haiti
Date Joined: 2007
Apostolic Leader: Lesly and Bernadette Bertrand

The Lord's Sanctuary Churches and Ministries
Location: Nakuru, Kenya
Date Joined: 2008
Apostolic Leader: Patrick and Nancy Thuo

Agrupacion Familiar Cristiana
Location: Mexico City, Mexico
Date Joined: 2009
Apostolic Leader: Gerardo and Fernanda Urena

Rays of Peace
Location: Karnataka State, India
Date Joined: 2015
Apostolic Leader: Mark Jayakumar

CityLights Churches
Location: Ubonratchathani, Thailand
A developing network under Hopewell Missions
The CityLights church plant started meeting in
    Ubon in 2014
Apostolic Leader: Lazaro and Merrilee Barrera

Bibliography

Cited Sources

1. Quam, Paula. (2014, July 1). Strawberry Lake: Christian Retreat and Conference Center celebrates 50 years of faith. DL Newspapers. Retrieved from http://www.dl-online.com/

2. A Survey of Biblical Teaching on the Holy Spirit by Merle G. Stoltzfus

3. Koch, Roy S. (1985, April) Mennonites Set Fire. *Christian Life.* p. 56

4. Koch, Roy S. (1985, April) Mennonites Set Fire. *Christian Life.* p. 57

5. Engle, Lou and Paine, Catherine. (1998) *Digging the Wells of Revival: Reclaiming Your Historic Inheritance Through Prophetic Intercession.* Destiny Image Publishers, Shippensburg, PA.

6. Sheets, Dutch. (2015, August 24) Re-digging the Wells of Revival: My Visits to Cane Ridge and Wales. Retrieved from https://www.dutchsheets.org/re-digging-the-wells-of-revival/

7. Hopewell Network of Churches Vision and Values, Confession of Faith dated 2015

Non-Cited Sources

Published Sources

Herskowitz, Linda S. (June 12th, 1978) *The Rebirth of a Born-Again Bar. Philadelphia Inquirer.* 1-B, 3-B

Horsch, John. (1917) *Infant baptism: its origin among Protestants and the arguments advanced for and against it.* Original publication, Scottsdale, PA. Reproduced by New York Public Library in 2011.

Lingg, Tory. (1977, October, 26) Elverson To Go Dry Nov. 1. *The Herald.* Honeybrook, PA.

Mast, J. Lemar & Mast, Lois Ann. (1982) *As Long As Wood Grows And Water Flows: A History of the Conestoga Mennonite Church.* Published by the Conestoga Mennonite Historical Committee. Tursack Printing, Inc. Pottstown, PA.

Synan, Vinson. (2001) *The Century of the Holy Spirit: 100 Years of Pentecostal and Charismatic Renewal, 1901 – 2001.* Thomas Nelson Publishers, Nashville, TN.

Zimmerman, Lester. (2012) *A Barn for the Harvest: Thirty Years of Faithfulness: The Story of Petra Christian Fellowship.* Petra Christian Fellowship. New Holland, PA.

Internet sources

Essential Anabaptist Mennonite Doctrines and Practices. (2010, May 23) Retrieved from http://www.anabaptists.org/doctrine.html

Acknowledgments

We could not have compiled this history without the help and input of many long-time members. First of all, we would like to recognize Truman Hertzler, Audrey Hanlon and Marie E. Cutman, who compiled the very helpful document entitled, Hopewell—Church With A History.

We would also like to thank the following people for sharing their memories, clippings, and other historical documents:

Mark Kraybill
Charlie Martin
John and Sandra Shantz
Johnny and Lilly Stoltzfus
Anita Wissinger
Kel and Pat Zook

For more information on the Hopewell Network, please visit:

HopewellNetwork.org